AN ANTHOLOGY OF POETRY
BY
YOUNG AMERICANS

1993 EDITION
VOLUME XL

Published by The American Academy of Poetry

The American Academy of Poetry
148 Sunset Avenue
Asheboro, NC   27203

Authors responsible for originality of poems
submitted.

ISBN: 1-883931-002

The American Academy of Poetry is dedicated to the beauty, self-expression, and fun of poetry. Prose just can't provide the musical rhythmic sounds or the strange and wonderfully quick images of poetry. This edition is filled with the emotions and imaginings of young poets. The subjects range from pets to world politics, from environmental concerns to just plain fun. The editors at the American Academy of Poetry were very impressed with quality of the poems and hope you enjoy reading them as much as we enjoyed putting this edition together.

The Editors

CHRISTMAS IS HERE

Christmas is here,
Everyone opening up presents,
Screaming and yelling from what they got,
Santa comes every year to fill your
stocking up.
In hopes he will come back the next year,
They sleep really tight,
All snuggled in their beds,
Dreaming of their presents.

Tony Hayden

REMARRIAGE

Putting two families together is like

Sticking together two pieces
of different colored paper

And expecting them to turn the
same color.

But...

If the families are like paints
They can blend together
to make a new color.

Lisa Plantenga
Age: 10

Witches flying through the air
Chilly wind whips through your hair.
Ghosts and spirits everywhere
Midnight
Hunter's teeth are sharp and bright.
As he stalks into the night
Victims scream with terror and fright.
1 O'clock
The dead have wept and shed their tears
Searching for their long lost dears.
The worst of all your greatest fears,
2 O'clock
Floorboards creak and shutters
clank
In the house its dark and
dank.
You thought all the spirits sank...
but they didn't.
3 O'clock
Goblins dance with joy and glee
Oh, at last they're finally free!
Around every corner and every tree.
they hide.
4 O'clock
Skeleton...knock, knock, tap
While you take a little nap.
Skeleton right in your lap.
5 O'clock
One hour left before they go
No trace left...nobody will know.
That they put on a little show.
6 O'clock

Gwyn Zawisza
Age: 11

2

FALL

It's fall.

It's fall when the leaves

are down,

and combines

are all around,

when pumpkins are orange,

when corn is brown,

and frost is all around.

Craig Sands
Age: 10

WINTER

With beauty and grace,
It comes down softly.
Not a sound is heard
Till children come out and
Enter a new world of fun.
Run and play children, run and play.

Meryl Ann Florance
Age: 11

LOVING

Loving is nice in good care
But good loving is very, very rare!

Ryan Haste
Age: 10

THE INDIAN

A very old and tall Indian sitting on
the stump.
A very wise old man,
who never feels pain in his rump,
for he will always make a stand.

He is very good in math.
This helps him to mark his way.
A perfect angle south for his path.
He has to now find a new place to stay.

He doesn't mind to find a new place.
He knows that he doesn't have to work fast,
for he remembers that it's not a race,
like it was in the past.

The wise old guy
will always have an open eye.

Larry Jordan
Age: 13

SNOW FLAKE

Falls slowly to the ground
melts very fast
cold as ice

Brad Devers
Age: 10

THE DOG

Once there was a dog
who sat on a log.
A toad came by
and sang a lullaby.
The dog fell asleep.
As far as I know the dog is still asleep!

Carla Deno
Age: 10

ROVER

My dog's name is Rover.
He's soft and furry all over.
He's as cute as sugar babies.
Too bad my dog has rabies!

Matt Dombroski
Age: 10

MICE

Mice like cheese.
They say please.
Mice like spice.
It's mighty nice.

Justin Burch
Age: 9

A GOAT

There was an old goat
Who ate all his oats.
Then his stomach did bloat
And ruffle his coat.
That was the end of the old
BILLY GOAT.

Jennifer Leighann Estes
Age: 8

MY BEST FRIEND

My best friend is Jenny.
She likes to collect pennies.
We run, we jump, we like to play.
We always say, 'What a beautiful day.

Lindsay Ross
Age: 9

THE TRUCK

Once upon a time
There was a truck,
That needed tires.
He wanted them put on with
PLIERS.

Christopher Hill
Age: 8

'ON HALLOWEEN NIGHT'

On Halloween night
I had a big fright.
I saw a coven of witches
All sitting in ditches.

They stoke a cache of jewels
Sitting on humped mules
They ate bananas
And put on bandannas.

They sat by trees
And got stung by bees
Now that they're gone
I won't need my wand.

Candi Harmon
Age: 9

I'M A QUEEN

I'm a queen with a crown.
But it keeps falling down.
My mom had sewn it to my head
with a thread.
It didn't do any good.
So, well...I had to wear a hood!

Sarah Datzman
Age: 10

BLUE

Blue is the ocean,
Where all the fish live and swim.
Without blue no one would have a notion
Blue is the sky,
Seeing birds fly by.
Blue feels like a blanket covering
the sky.
Blue taste like blueberries that
have just been picked.
Blue smells like the ocean big
and wide.
So if you touch it, it's as light
as a feather.

Jeffrey Maresh
Age: 9

THINGS THAT WIGGLE AND JIGGLE

There once was a frog who swallowed a fly.
He wiggled and jiggled across the sky.

There once was a cat who swallowed a hat.
He wiggled and jiggled across the mat.

There once was a hog who swallowed a dog.
He wiggled and jiggled across a log.

Amber Barton
Age: 8

APRIL

April, Oh, April, are you here yet?
April, Oh, April, I hope you're all wet.
April, Oh, April when all flowers bloom.
April, Oh, April you smell like perfume.
April, Oh, April you're the best of all days.
April, Oh, April my birthday in you.
April, Oh, April you're the cure of the flu.
April, Oh, April I love the songs you sing.
April, Oh, April when the school bell does not ring.

Robin Thada
Age: 9

THE COLOR BLUE

The color blue is a blue jay high in the sky.
It's blueberries, It's even little blue fairies.
Blue is a Nile blue as the sky.
Blue smells cool like a winter's day.
They're like blue butterflys some people say.

It tastes cold like ice but it's rather nice.
It feels like a pillow, a bright blue one.
It makes you feel sad and that's not much fun.
I like blue.
I think you should too.

Chelsea Harris
Age: 10

CHRIST WAS BORN

Christ was born
He was born in a barn
Three wise men came
And gave him fragrances
He was all nice and warm
Animals all around him
There he lay asleep
He grew old then
Gave his life for you and me
Then he rose again 3 days later
Now he promises to come
and save us to take us to heaven.

Jessica R. Crum
Age: 11

THE SHOE

There once was a boy who lived in a shoe.
And I'll tell you something, this shoe wasn't
blue.
He went to Mars
and went in a car.
While he was gone his shoe changed to blue.
So when he got back he found down in the
ground a piece of his blue shoe.

Carly Ward
Age: 10

BATH WATER WHITE

Bath water white
is so clean when
it's running.
Bath water white
sounds like tinkle
swiss, tinkle, swiss.
When soap is in
bath water, it turns
bath water white
to bath water yellow.

Bath water white
is a white cover
of night.
Bath water white
feels like liquid
paper 'poofed'
into square paper.
Bath water white
tastes like 'plain
old water'
Bath water white
smells like 'dew' on a
fresh summer morning,
or snow on a winter's
day.
Bath water white
is gentle and timid,
one touch of a finger nail
makes it shiver.

Bath water white.

Lindsey Forbes
Age: 9

CHRISTMAS

Joyful and cold ALL toys in stores are sold.
Your mother has told,
The stories of the old
St. Nick.
You hang your stocking low,
For the slow bold St. Nick,
For if you hang them high
The poor St. Nick will have to fly,
And then he may get a sty on his eye
He carries a bag,
That always sags,
He puts down the bag that always sags
And brings out the toys,
For little tiny girls and boys.
Under the tree the toys will await
sort of a bait,
For little children know
Off Santa goes with a blanket over his toes,
Ready to go home till next Christmas.

Jeremy Michael Fitzgerald
Age: 10

MY CAT

My cat loves me.
My cat cares.
My cat likes to
Run down stairs.
My cat purrs.
My cat meows.
My cat and I are very best pals!

My cat is silly.
My cat is nice.
My cat likes to
Hunt down mice.
My cat jumps.
My cat falls.
My cat enjoys
Playing with balls.
My cat itches.
My cat scratched.
My cat and I
Deserve a pat on the back!

My cat is cool.
My cat is neat.
My cat always
Washes her feet.
She also has
To wash her seat!

My cat bites.
My cat claws.
My cat kicked me
In the jaws!
My cat knows

It's okay
Because she's only
Doing it for play!

Katelin Reeves
Age: 10

TEACHERS

Teachers are strict
and daring.
But yet they're funny
and caring.
And they give you homework.
But that's how teachers do their work.

Elaina Brooke Jones
Age: 10

NOVEMBER

November is a time for fun
November is a time for love
November is a time to thank
The people who found the
United States.

Eric Brown
Age: 11

FOOTBALL

Football is a rough sport!
They play and play and play.
And when they stop
They get smashed! Just like that.
They don't know why they play
that sport.
Some get hurt and some don't.
They just play that sport like
that! Will they ever stop? I
don't know.

Blake Thornsbrough
Age: 10

AUTUMN

Autumn is coming.
The leaves are turning brown.
The turkeys in the oven
just turning round and round.
Oh what a wonderful day!
What a wonderful day!
Autumn is here
And it's Thanksgiving Day!

Stephanie Ellis
Age: 10

FALL LEAVES

Fall
Leaves Me
Happy in the
Cold times of weather
But in the cold times
Of weather the leaves
Turn different colors
Oh I wish that it
was fall now so I could
jump into the leaves

Gordon Hansen
Age: 10

LEAVES AND FALL

Leaves come
in many colors
Like red,
green, yellow,
orange, and
brown.
Fall with many colors, and corn
pumpkin, tomatoes, and apples.

Dawn Grimes
Age: 10

17

THE CIRCUS

Horses leap and jump.
Horses glide through the air.
Hoofs clickity clumb
As they are placed with care.

People waiting around
As the horses enter the ring.
Popcorn and candy around
As the clowns are starting to sing.

I can't wait, can't wait
Until the show starts.
The main clown is late.
Will he break our hearts?

Here comes the beautiful horse.
Here comes the happy clown.
Don't know where they were, of course
I'm happy they were found.

Heather Zahn
Age: 13

GRACE

I have not seen Grace in over a year
And somehow I haven't shed a tear.
I miss her so, don't you see?
I want her to be right here with me.
I miss her so much.
She misses me, too. I hope ....
But I feel like I'm hanging
from a very weak rope.

I call her everyday just to say 'Hi'
And when I do, it feels like I'm flying
in the sky!

It feels good to talk to her, and it should.
She's a very good friend,
following all the new fashion trends.
Every time I look at her picture in my mind,
It feels like there is something new to find.
She's a very good person!
My friend, too ....
And someday, I hope she can
meet you, too!

Allison Dormer
Age: 9

DUSK

The sun sets by the
water with the sky red, pink.
Birds sleep peacefully.

Brendea Wright
Age: 10

TOYLAND

Toyland is where all dreams come true.
It's like a place you never knew.
It's a place where fairy tales live,
But what may be better than that is to give.
To others not so fortunate as you and me,
So that all of us could share in a Toyland
dream.
And all of us happy be.

Stephanie Scipione
Age: 9

FLIGHT

The tree covers the
sun when it is setting and
all the birds go home.

Matthew Brennan
Age: 9

MASTERPIECE

A painter takes the sun
and turns it into a
yellow spot.

An artist takes the yellow
spot and turns it
into the sun.

Suzanne Marguerite Morrison
Age: 9

WHISPER

The whisper of the
grass in the old green meadow
is pretty music.

Naomi Cutler
Age: 9

BEST FRIENDS

Friends are something you never want
To lose just like a flower so sweet.
They make you laugh they cry.
So never lose your friends they're
too precious.

Jalyn Bowen
Age: 11

IF I WERE A DINOSAUR

If I were a dinosaur
I would be a carnivore

Or maybe I'd be ultrasaur
Then I'd be more than
50 floors.

I would be the color pink
then again, I'd be extinct.

What else could I be?
Oh, let me think
Oh, let me see.

Maybe I won't be a dinosaur
maybe I'll just be me.

Jennifer Harrold
Age: 8

FISH

F for fins helps fish swim
I for water insects that fish eat
S for scales slimy too
H abitat that everything has
   but what about you?

Alec Hershman
Age: 7

MATH

Why do we have to do Math?
Math, it doesn't make sense to me!
I'd much rather take a warm bath.
Or take a ride in the roaring sea.

Why do we need to know how wide,
A rectangle or square may be?
The answer may be suicide.
Jumping off a bridge the end be.

How awful is the subject of math!
You hope to get locked in the bathroom!
To miss all the fury and wrath.
The subject of math, a horrible doom!

We should all skip math class.
I would rather be baking dough.
Bribing in order to pass!
The thing I hate most, it goes slow.

David Dolak
Age: 12

HOBBIES

My hobby is reading.
My hobby is math.
My hobby is riding a
Horse down a path.
Some hobbies are different,
Some are the same.
Some hobbies just come,
Some already came.
Lots of hobbies are great,
One's perfectly fine.
And I know a person who has
Eighty-nine!

Colleen Collins
Age: 8

MY DOG

I ran out to him and he barked as if a word
and I listened with my heart.
It seemed as he was saying he loved me with
his heart.

To hear you have to listen with your heart.
It might be difficult but you will get the
hang of it if you just try hard.

Rachel Brainerd
Age: 6

GROWING UP

Become an adult
Think not about the dream
Forget your childhood.
And the wings that you soared with
When you were a child.

Sarah Fertig
Age: 7

ICE CREAM

Ice cream, Ice cream in a dish,
How many scoops do you wish?
Millions of flavors try one and savor.
Slurp it, burp it, take your pick,
Go ahead have a lick!

Kara Wenzel
Age: 10

THINGS IN MARIO LAND

Goombas,
Bloopers,
Koopa-
Troopers

Ba-bombs blast
Bullet's bang
Hammer's thrown
and boomerangs

Turtle shells,
Robot dolls,
Magic leaves,
and fire balls

There is a hero
his name, Mario
He's got an evil twin
Nasty Wario.

Jon Wallace
Age: 10

OCEAN

I've always wanted to be the ocean,
cradling life...
My breath taking power, destroying, but
yet preserving.
Strength so great not even a mountain
dare challenge me...
But so graceful, so graceful not to move a
grain of sand from my floor.
A flick of my wrist, uncovers natural
treasures.
The moon compliments me on my blinding
morning shine...
As the fishermen complain of my bitter
spray.
My afternoons filled with surfers tickling
my back...and children stealing my shells.
Best of all the evening calm with gulls
resting on my lazy waves...
With the wind singing me to sleep, to sleep,
to sleep...

Carrie Bock
Age: 11

Pascal
Boy, smart
Running, playing, escaping
Like a best friend
Pupil

Steven Bragg
Age: 8

THOUGHTS

It's always better to say it
than to leave a thought unsaid.
It thus can be digested
with truest meaning read.

Words can express our truest thought
and give our thought true meaning.
Imagination left at work has trouble bought,
oft toward distortion leaning.

When we express just what we mean
no matter how it's taken,
We escape the danger of another's thought
oft our thoughts unmaking.

So think your thoughts
Express them true
and they will do
good work for you.

Danielle Oliverio
Age: 13

Balloon
red, blue
flying, floating, popping
like a good friend
a floating ball with string

Ben Zurawski
Age: 8

HAPPY FEET

Shopping is so cool,
I go after school.

I look for the sales,
Inside Bloomingdales.

Shoes and skirts and tops,
Are in all the shops.

Going to the mall,
Can be fun for all.

There are lots of floors,
Also lots of stores.

Time goes by so fast,
I go home at last.

Rachelle M. Rotunda
Age: 11

Balloon
Red Pretty
Flying floating turning
like a magic kite
ball

Mariam Kassem
Age: 8

I HAVE A CAT

I have a cat - her name is Sam.
Wherever she goes, she gets in a jam.
She has blue eyes and her paws are brown
And when she hides, she cannot be found.
So don't say I didn't warn you -
Don't say it please,
When my mother didn't warn me,
She bit off my sleeve.

Lindsey Marie Hill
Age: 8

Balloon
blue fun
playing popping flying
like a flying bird
friend

Albert Zhuli
Age: 8

THE PLACE

Do you know this place? I know
this magic place you can go
The place where Fairies glow
And the magic mushrooms grow?
I can show you this place to
go. If you can know all that you
can know and then so you can go to
this place I know.

Tim Stecker
Age: 14

Balloon
bouncy red
following floating telling
like a triangle kite
airship

Ali Boomrod
Age: 8

BASKETBALL

Basketball is fun,
It's a game that makes you run.
You hear the crowd roar.
As you come through the door.
You score while you,
run up and down the floor.

Matthew Booe
Age: 10

THIS TOOTH

I jiggled it
jaggled it
jerked it.

I pushed
and pulled
and poked it.

But --

As soon as I stopped
and left it alone.
This tooth came out
on its very own!

Reema Rayan
Age: 9

WHY?

Why do people care? Why?
Why do we learn?
Why do we have to pay a fare?
Why do we have ferns?
Why do we breathe air?
Because God made those things,
And that's life.

Molly Lindamood
Age: 10

IF I WERE IN CHARGE OF THE WORLD

If I were in charge of the world.
I'd let kids rule their country.
Ice cream wouldn't be fattening.
Everyone would be friends.
Nobody would starve.
Everybody would have at least one
million dollars.
I would make sure there was no war.
I would pay all taxes for everyone.
Cars would fly on air.
Everything I wish would come true.
It would always be summer.

Nora Hamdan
Age: 9

GIFTS ARE...

Gifts are better than the best.
It's a gift to hear a bird sing,
To hear its soft voice ring,
Breaking through the silence of the day.
It's a gift to feel the summer sun,
Or to feel the coldness of winter.
Yes, a gift is better
Than the best.

Jaime Kathleen Bugaski
Age: 9

IF I WERE IN CHARGE OF THE WORLD

If I were in charge of the world,
I'd like to see the oceans and the rivers
clean.
We would like to see people in peace.
Children would like to see the poor people
have something to eat.
I could give money to every one in the world.
Everyone would like to see their children
like each other.
I would cancel smoking.
We would save the rain forest.
A world without disease.

Huda Elkhazendar
Age: 9

I saw a poor man
walking down the street.
Wearing clothes all ripped,
no shoes on his feet.
His face was all dirty.
His hair all a mess.
He would try to steal money,
get caught - and confess.
So many people
have to live this way.
But as you pass them,
What is there to say?

Lauren Kovach
Age: 10

THE WILD GEESE

When they sense the
coming of winter they
leave to go down south.

When they sense the
coming of spring, they
come back north again.

This happens every year
when the winter comes and
winter goes. The Wild
Geese will always know.

Melissa Motylinski
Age: 12

KITTENS

There was a kitten
That was as white
As snow and
You could
Even see
It in the
Night.

Amanda Contreras
Age: 11

THE TWELVE MONTHS

January: Wintry winds blowing so cold,
A jolly snowman, what a sight to behold.

February: Happy Valentine's Day,
It is such a lovely thing to say.

March: Beautiful trees and flowers growing,
In my face, warm winds are blowing.

April: Wonderful sprinkles of rain,
Making pitter-patter noises on my window pane.

May: Tulips, daisies and other flowers,
Grow happily after April showers.

June: School's out, all the kids cheer,
But only a few have a tear.

July: Hot winds making a soft silent sound,
With kites flying all around.

August: Swimming, camping, and all that fun,
Also laying out in the warm, shining sun.

September: School starts all the kids cry,
While summer activities say good-bye.

October: Red, orange, yellow, and green,
Look at all the colors that can be seen.

November: Squirrels gather nuts and other
stuff, so their winter stay won't be so tough.

December: Chilling winds blowing in my face.
Christmas gifts wrapped with lace.

Andrew Ballnik
Age: 12

IF I WERE IN CHARGE OF THE WORLD

If I were in charge of the world.
Swing sets would be five feet higher.
Arcade games would be free.
Rain would be hot chocolate.
Animals could talk like humans.
People could fly like an eagle or falcon.
A bird would lay golden eggs.
Nobody would be fat only skinny.
Kids could get their license.
Snow would be whipped cream.
Everybody would be rich.
A Lamborghini would be two dollars.
Windows would slide up and down easier.
You would get ten dollars every day.
GI Joe guys would come alive.
Shoes would be metal or steal.
Shirts could not get stained.
People could come out of your TV.
Invisible tape would stick better.

Joseph Byrne
Age: 8

SUMMER ON AN ISLAND

In the summer I lived on an island alone.
I would send messages in bottles instead
   of by phone.
I would build a fire to keep away the cold.
The trees I use for firewood are old.
Sometimes people come see my sand-
   castles by boat.
My island is surrounded by water like
   my sand castles are by a moat.
The fish I catch are very pretty.
And at the end of the summer I go
   to my home in the city.

Jeremy Rutkowski
Age: 9

I AM THANKFUL FOR...

I am thankful for my voice.
God made a good choice.
I am thankful for my mother
'cause I really love her.
I am thankful for my father.
I am glad I am his daughter.
I am thankful for my sister
'cause sometimes she will let me kiss her.

Michelle Bower
Age: 10

'GOLDEN AFTERNOON'

The Morning Glories are taking their nap,
while the caterpillars are sucking sap,
the lengthy daisies make the flowers swoon
  on a golden afternoon.
The spiders spin a silvery quilt,
the heart-broken flowers really wilt,
you'll forget this place, but oh, how soon,
  on a golden afternoon.

Mike Massey
Age: 11

DON'T SAY FRIGHT

It was a scary October night; when someone
said the word fright.
The winds were blowing; it was raining too.
That's why it may have scared you.
There was a knocking at the door;
so I got down on the floor.
It broke into the house, and I ran
faster than a mouse.
I fainted by the bed, and it must have
thought I was dead; for
at that moment it left, and never came
back again.

Bruce G. Warren
Age: 11

SNOW

I love the snow in
wintertime,
The flakes are pearl
and white.
And when it drifts
upon the land,
It makes the whole
world bright.
But best of all is
when it's deep,
Up to our very noses,
And I go out and play all day.
Because my school
always closes.

Carrie Amenson
Age: 10

RAIN

Rain, pit, pat, pit, pat,
It brings happiness to my heart.
Rain is beautiful music to my ears.
Then it strikes,
   BOOM!
Thunder & lightning!
But the rain starts it's wonderful
Pit, pat, pit, pat again!

Jennifer Seguin
Age: 10

42

MY CAT

My friend and my
companion my
friend to keep me
company. He chases
a lot of mice
I'll tell you he
is nice.
My cat and my
friend, my friend
to keep me
company. He plays
with me when I am
sad. He still loves
when I am mad.

Jessica Glowacki
Age: 8

TRAINS

The train that runs through the night,
From dusk till dawn with just one light.

The light will shine where people gather,
To ride the train if they'd rather.

So take the train there and back
You're sure to stay on the right track.

Randy Read
Age: 11

FALL

Fall is a beautiful season.
The leaves change color on
the trees.
When the wind comes
the leaves fall to the ground.
And, create a blanket of color.
We rake the leaves into a pile
and, jump in them.
When we jump in the pile
of leaves,
They all fly up in the air
and slowly fall down on top
of your head.

Emily Scott
Age: 12

AUSTRALIA

It is my favorite country.
It wasn't then, but now.
You probably wonder why,
You probably wonder how.

It's a country, continent, island
All at the same time.
I'll move there when I'm all grown-up,
I know Australia's mine!

Emily Glowacki
Age: 9

THE DOG AND THE CAT

The dog was laughing
at the cat.
The cat was sitting
on a big mat.
The cat got upset
and started to cry.
The dog fell for it
because the cat was so sly.
The dog came over to apologize.
But the cat was famous
for her lies.

Christina Michelle Vergolini
Age: 13

FRIENDS

Friends are nice
When you need them.
Friends are nice
When you need them.
Friends are nice
When you share.
But friends are not nice
If they give you a scare.

Ben Lanehart
Age: 11

WHAT DO I DO?

What do I do?
She wants me to clean my room!
Dust it, vacuum, put it all away.
Or throw it in the closet for another day.
Push it, shove it under the bed.
Or watch TV. standing on my head.
What do I do?
She gave me an hour or was it two!
Put all the junk in a box.
Put all the clothes with the socks.
Or throw it all down the chute.
Down, down it goes.
Watch the expression on her face
As it all disappears without a trace!

Anna Schweickart
Age: 13

SLEEPOVER

The girls play games,
The girls watch TV.
They get on their pajamas.
They went into bed and giggled.
In the morning they eat.
Then they change, and talk.
They had a wonderful sleepover.
They had a wonderful sleepover.

Theresa Hartka
Age: 12

MY PET

My pet is funny,
my pet did not cost me any money.

My pet is short, but very sweet,
and he loves to play with my feet.

My pet, look what he can do,
he can jump up and down,
and can do tricks too.

My pet is my best friend,
my pet he will stay with me
through thick and thin.

Crystal Varney
Age: 10

FRIENDS LOST

Last night I lay awake in bed,
Sadness floating in my head.
About the times when friends repelled,
When my happiness flatly fell.
Emily said mean things to me,
Alicia didn't give a care for me.
I know I'm lucky to have a friend,
But who knows what's around the bend.

Erin Trussell
Age: 9

SUICIDE

A friend of our family just passed away,
He committed suicide last Sunday.

His parents went to church and left him at
home,
When they came back, he was dead in his room.

They found him with a gun in his hand
His father had bought from another land.

They called an ambulance to take him away,
I have not seen him since that day.

There was a funeral for only his family,
After the funeral, he was buried in a
cemetery.

I cried a long time when I heard the news,
I thought he was drunk from drinking
booze.

I found out he had a fight with his
girlfriend,
He decided to take matters into his own
hands.

He was twenty at the time, but used to
play GI Joe with my brother.
When he died he didn't realize all those
who would suffer.

Just because life isn't the way you want
it to be,

Doesn't mean suicide is the right thing
for you or me.

Try to work things out in the problem
you have,
Everyone has one chance at life, two
if lucky.

Sarah Kristensen
Age: 13

CHRISTMAS AND WINTER

The trees outside have no leaves.
And through the air is a chilly breeze.
Children make angels in the snow,
We can't wait for Christmas though!
Santa comes with help and care,
He give toys to children who are nice,
And share.
We waited and waited for Santa to come,
We looked at the cookies and wanted some.
Then we heard something on the roof,
It was of course a reindeer hoof!
He looked at the gifts underneath the tree,
Then he turned his head and looked at me!
But, then he went and got on his sleigh,
And flew far, far, far, far away.
As he flew away on reindeer,
We knew that he'd be back next year!

Laura Senko
Age: 9

MY TREE

My tree is bright, beautiful, and serene.
The breeze rushes through the calm little tree
and whistles away that sweet song for me
each day.

For my tree is the only tree so special to me,
for I've searched land far and near for none
has that sweet sound that I hear in my ear.

My tree is so special and I treat it with care
for this little tree, my only tree,
I must share to be fair
with the land and the air.

Maeann DeMars
Age: 11

MY BABY BROTHER

My baby brother,
He loves my mother!
He kicks and cries,
While his diaper dries.
He always sobs,
When he opens the doorknobs.
My baby brother,
He loves by mother!

Angela Weaver
Age: 11

CHRISTMAS

Christmas, Christmas is a happy day.
Christmas is a joyful day.
Christmas is a holiday.
Christmas is when the snow falls from
the sky to the ground.
Christmas is a day where there are presents
under the tree.
Christmas is an important day.
Christmas is when people sing
and dance to the music.
Christmas is a time for happiness.
Christmas is when you decorate your tree
and your house inside and out.
Christmas is for memories of times.
Christmas is when children get out of
school for two weeks or more.
Christmas is the time where you leave out
cookies and milk for Santa Claus to eat
and drink.
Christmas is a time to be good not bad
or you won't get any presents.
Christmas is a time when Mom bakes cookies
in the oven to eat.
Christmas is a time where you play with
your toys after you open them.
Christmas!!!!

Heather Ringer

SUNSHINE, MOONLIGHT

I see the sunshine,
Rise in the east.
I see the sunshine,
Set in the west.

I see the moonlight,
Rise up from the ground.
I see the moonlight,
Set where it's never found.

Now what does all this mean?,
It means that God made the world,
the sun, and the moon.

For all that is told,
Will surely come true.

Monica Trygg

SADNESS

Sadness is when you need a friend,
Someone you can count on,
Someone who won't pretend,
They will be a real friend.
I think my friends are someone like that
But some are not.

Jenni Forgette

Lightning
On a rainy day
In the sky
Electric volts
To release energy.

Brian Donald Adams
Age: 11

MY MOM MARRIED THE PRINCIPAL

My Mom married the principal the first day in
May,
Oh dear, Oh, dear, What will my classmates
say?
My Mom told her very best friend,
And then I knew it was the end.
The very next day I went to school,
And boy, did I feel like a fool.
Everyone in the whole school found out,
And the word was going about.
I could hardly believe my ears when someone
said:
I think to have the principal as a dad would
be neat,
I bet you'll be the most popular person on
your street.
Maybe having the principal as a dad,
Isn't all that bad.

Maria Kallis
Age: 9

COLORS, IMAGINE THAT...

Imagine that I am a brilliant gold,
excitement shining through,
just as sunlight filters through clear glass.
The sun's rays dance among despairing
shadows spreading eagerness and hope.

Imagine that I am a bold red,
a fire burning deep within,
seizing control of all other emotions.
Scorching sensitivity of others while masked
with my shocking, destructive anger.

Imagine that I am the purest white,
a glistening cloud dripping with crystal
wishes.
A misplaced angel upon the earth
with not a thought of disguising
my innocence or honesty.

Imagine that I am only pools of melancholy
blue,
filled with tears symbolizing my great
sadness.
Rippling waters washing away all confusion,
exposing the truth of heart and soul
while drowning all other thoughts.

Imagine that I am a jade green,
playful and prankish, taunting and
teasing,
cavorting and capering, frolicking
and frisking.
Mischievously mocking the seriousness

of the world.

Imagine that I am a rosy mauve,
a bursting flower in the sunset skies,
an untouchable, whimsical dream.
My immense feeling of contentment is
a blanket of warmth enveloping all.

Imagine that I am the coldest black,
dark and fearsome, void of emotion,
yearning for freedom from a pit a
devastation.
Searching for peace of mind, forever
hoping to find
a dream that will not shatter.

Imagine that I am a prism,
a reflective jewel, grasping all
colors,
shining a beam of light, so strong,
so powerful.
Amazing is this gift of love,
that is born of all emotions.

Elizabeth Mihalo
Age: 12

DESERT

Desert
Warm and quiet,
The cactuses blooming
I get feelings of peacefulness.
My place.

Carrie Baran
Age: 12

THE WAY THAT THE WIND BLOWS

The wind blows in a gentle way,
or a rough way;
Wind blows fast or slow and sometimes
you can't feel it;
When you feel the wind,
it feels like someone is breathing on you;
When the wind blows gentle,
it feels like a fan on low;
When the wind blows rough,
it feels like an airplane right above you;
When the wind blows fast,
it feels like when you run and the wind
is hitting your face;
When the wind blows slow,
it feels like a baby touching you;
That is the way that the wind sometimes blows
and sometimes feels.

David Jason Webb
Age: 11

The sun is glowing and burning
bright like a ball of fire.
Yellow with light making things grow,
giving off its energy
With its big bright yellow glow.

Kelly Mann
Age: 11

JUST ME

Feel nothing for me for I am supposedly
strong.
Feel nothing for me because I always belong.
Feel nothing for me, I'm a star out in space,
Feel nothing for me, pretend I'm not looking
at your face.

There are people who care and people who don't,
people who live and people who won't.
Will somebody love me?
Somewhere out there?

Is there someone with feelings like mine to share?
If there's someone to love me, please speak up.
Someone to comfort me when I'm mad and hug me
when I'm sad.
If you're out there, please come and visit me,
I'll be in the orphanage window, you see.

Lyndsay Hage
Age: 11

AUTUMN

The world is so colorful when it is Fall,
The color can amaze anyone at all,
The leaves fall down, all the way to the
ground,
People rake them up and jump around.

Lacey Grenier
Age: 10

PIGS

Pigs are cute, small, long,
Short, big, thin.
Their noses are like a little cup.
I can go on, on, on.
Pinky is my name.

Deboah Grabski
Age: 11

CHRISTMAS

Christmas
Tinsel, happy
Unwrapping, "thank you"s, play
Families receive and give presents
Noel

Andrea Brophy
Age: 11

Inside
Warm, comfortable
Laying in bed
Safe, calm, loud, cold
Smelly, noisy, boring, sickening
Dirty, dangerous
Outside

Jason Blakeley
Age: 12

THE GREAT AMERICAN GAME

The pitcher winds up and pitches
the ball.
Everyone sits nervously awaiting
the call.

'Strike one!' yells the ump loud
and clear.
From the batter he gets an
ugly sneer.

The next pitch is a called strike
and everyone knows,
The batter has to hit this one
with a mighty blow.

The bases are loaded, there are
two outs.
The pitcher lets go of the ball as the
crowd lets up a shout.

Around comes the batter, he hits
it hard, it's a grand slam! He did it!
We've won the World Series
with that hit!

This game has been a tiring
bout,
But this is what baseball is
all about.

Andrea Rahaley
Age: 12

THANKSGIVING

Tricks
Hens
Apples
Nest
Kids
Sun
Giving
Indians
Victory
Ice
November
Grandparents!

Rachel Sherzer
Age: 8

THE MOON

The moon is yellow
The moon is bright
The moon is shining
All through the night.

The moon comes out
Very, very soon
The moon comes out
Every afternoon.

Scott Allison

MONSTERS?

Lying in my bed,
  Can't sleep at all.
There's not any noise
  In the creepy hall.
I'm walking in the hall;
  I don't hear a sound,
But suddenly I hear footsteps,
  So I quickly turn around.
I look and see a monster
  Scarier than a bear.
Oh, I guess it's not a monster.
  It's my brother with wacky hair!

Amy Sherron
Age: 9

Friends are nice
They're there when you need them,
when you need them the most.
They make you laugh,
when you're sad or gloomy.
They take you places,
When you need to get away.
They send you cards,
When you're sick and in bed.
I think,
The world is a better place because we
have friends like that.

Brianna Addley
Age: 11

WILD HOOVES

Their wild hooves pound upon the ground.

Their ear-splitting sound will amaze you.

And their beauty and grace, which is when they
give chase,

Is surely ready to change you.

If I shout with glee,

They'll suddenly flee

For they are afraid of me.

So if they see you a hidin',

The horse you were riding,

They're grateful that they are the free.

Jennifer Gumas
Age: 9

ROSES ARE RED

Roses are red, violets are blue,
For I'm going to scare you, boo.

Roses are red, violets are blue,
Happy Valentines Day from me to you.

Roses are red, violets are blue,
Don't look at me I'm lost too.

Roses are red, violets are blue,
For I don't have a clue.

Roses are red, violets are blue,
I shall stick to you like glue.

Roses are red, violets are blue,
Don't eat me I'm eating beef stew.

Kendra Parker
Age: 9

LEAVES

Leaves
Colorful, pretty
Falling, growing, rustling
Happy, lovable, sad, nice
Leaves.

Stephen Favor
Age: 8

MY DESK

My desk is a mess.
It isn't the best
And out of school
It's worse than the rest.

It's filled with fries
And strawberry pie,
Tennis shoes, banana peels,
And some old, dusty flies.

A tennis racquet
And a matchbox car,
A jar of honey
And a broken guitar.

A rotten apple
From yesterday's lunch
A Snickers, a Milky Way,
And a Nestle Crunch.

A bottle of water
And my old lunch tray,
My desk is a mess,
That's all there is to say.

Brad Hill
Age: 11

ICICLES

I as in cold as ice
C as in freezing cold...burrrr
I as in icicles
C as in warm cocoa
L as in laughing in the snow
E as in eating yummy soup
S as in sledding d   hills
               o
                 w
                   n

Elizabeth Resovsky
Age: 12

FALL

F is the f
    a
     l
     l
      i
       n
        g leaves.
A is all the children playing
L is the colorful leaves
L is the lazy days that go...by.

Andrea J. Moses
Age: 11

SILVER MOON

As the moon sets out over the blue,
And the waves meet the land that they
never knew,
The moon up above with its face all a bright,
Splits through the darkness of the night,
Shadows are cast out on the water,
And a bright stream of light shines on the
sea otter,
He dives and swims showing only his playful
face,
Right now this is a magical place,
Soon the sun begins to break,
The moon is gone,
And now it is the break of dawn!

Adrienne Stephen
Age: 10

THE SUN

The sun, the sun, the big golden sun.
The sun warms and lights the earth
so we can have fun.
It floats high in the sky during the day.
It makes a beautiful sunset
then it goes away.
But it will come again another day.

Aaron Zvanciuk
Age: 11

BREAKING UP

Relief yet sorrow fills you.
Can you forget?
You can't shut out
The memories that have been hidden inside
for so long.
The memories that warmed you
on the coldest nights.
Admitting the problems and solving them
graciously.
Stating the facts and thoughts aloud
comforts you in the silence of morning.
Remembering the good and bad times.
The feeling you shared calms you
in the darkness of night;
Shuts out the sadness.
The arguments that left you weary.
You shout at the world for giving you
this misery.
Why, why me?
What happened to forgive and forget?
What happened to love?
Forgiving the past and enjoying the future.
That's what must be done.
But can I forgive that person?
That person that entered my life
and destroyed it by leaving?
Yes
Yes, I can.
Freedom.
A rebirth and a new beginning.

Dry your eyes after the destruction is over.
Love dies,
but also brings a brighter tomorrow.

Christy Crews
Age: 13

Hopeless cries of fear
Endless pain
Lonely until found
Pleading and begging for your life

Puncture or wound
Aching joints and muscles
Internal bleeding, feeling bad inside
Nothing to cure

Paul Szafarczyk
Age: 13

MOTHER NATURE

Mother nature
Colorful, pretty
Rainy, sunny, cloudy
Happy, nice, wonderful, beautiful
Mother nature

Lisa Bosley
Age: 8

THE PERFORMANCE

For ten years, a young girl practices
to be a dancer.
One month before the recital,
she finds out that she has a
crippling disease and is confined
to a wheelchair.
For one month, she lives the nightmare
of not being able to dance and hear
the applause of the audience.
The night of the performance, she is
wheeled out onto the stage.
As she tries to do steps in her wheelchair,
she looks out into the audience and realizes
that they cannot clap because they have
no hands.

Dawn Fagerland
Age: 13

Butterfly
Colorful, bright
Wings, pattern, fly
Soft, flowing, long, fat
Furry, slow, crawls
Cocoon, dull
Caterpillar

Nicole Morrone
Age: 11

OUR SKY

The big blue sky hovers above us,
Watching every single soul on the earth.

Like a blanket it protects us,
from the burning sun outside.

The sky has been there long before we have,
yet it accepts us, and takes care of us,
And we still continue to destroy it.

Amy Carnes
Age: 13

MORNING BY THE OCEAN

The morning sun gleams on the
water,
And in the ripples is a young sea otter.
The leaves on the palm rustle in the breeze,
While dolphins glide through the water with
the greatest of ease.
The shells on the beach lay undisturbed,
As the waves are singing without saying
a word.
The beauty keeps on, still and unbroken,
As if a spell has been awoken.

Laurie Eccles
Age: 10

THE LOVE

It's the love no one understands, the kind
that doesn't require trying. The love that
lies deep in the heart, blooming in every
season.

Each color of this love is bright and
full. The colors are unknown. It makes you
sing, it makes you smile and confuses you all
the while.

This love I feel isn't the same as one
between two. Yet it is deeper, more special
than special. The kind that will always be
in my heart.

It's the love that requires an emotional
price. I'm willing to pay, for that love.

Sarah Frankel
Age: 12

TREES

Trees sway and whistle all around the town.
The trees let leaves of all colors fall down.
They wave at people walking on the street.
The kids run around thinking the trees are
neat.
When the people are at home, the trees frown.

Suzanne Parker
Age: 13

FLOWERS

Flowers come in all different colors.
Flowers come in all different sizes.
Flowers are pretty.
Flowers are different.

Flowers come in all different sizes.
They bloom in spring or summers.
Flowers are different.
You don't have to plant seeds to see flowers.
People plant flowers near the house.

You can give them to some people.
Flowers are pretty.
People plant flowers near the house.
Flowers come in all different colors.

Elaine Wilbur
Age: 13

Christchild
Holly
Recite
Incense
Stable
The gifts
Muir
Animals
Shepherds

Matthew Murr
Age: 11

73

KRIS KRINGLE

Who's the man who comes each year,
That puts smiles on faces and brings good
cheer.

His name is Kris Kringle, the jolly old
fellow. For his heart is pure and his
thoughts are mellow.

He's as plump as a melon ready to pick.
Sometimes they call him Jolly Old St. Nick.

He only comes one day in December,
But that's a night we all remember.

Down the chimney his body does go,
Over to the tree, sprayed with snow.

He opens up his bag loaded with toys,
To give to all good girls and boys.

With a smile on his face and full of good
cheer, he places the presents that they
have waited for all year.

He grabs a cookie that was left for him,
And looks down at his belly that's not so
thin.

Then comes a roar of laughter and a Ho, Ho,
Ho, back up through the chimney and away he
goes.

All night long he flies through the sky,

Delivering presents and last good-byes.

For when the night is over, he goes home to
rest. Knowing that all children think he's
the best.

Dan Earl

White, a fresh new day.
A puffy cloud against
    the blue sky.
White, the wind with a
    dove on its back.
The sand on the shore or,
    the waves that crash.

White, the face of a
    frightened child.
A color that isn't, but is.
An angel watching with
    pale eyes over the starry nights.

White, is a castle on a hill,
A unicorn in the mist.
White, the reflection of all colors.
A brilliant sunset that
leads to the morning horizon.

Kim Belsley
Age: 13

LONELY

You watch your favorite celebrities
on the television set,
Watching all the ones you wish
you could have met,
Sitting on your hospital bed
while you dream you were at home,
Nobody comes to visit and you feel all alone.

Remembering all the times you had,
The things you did, both good and bad,
You grew up, and changed your ways,
But never forgot the good old days

You had two children that cried at night,
You put up with them even when they'd fight,
But soon they grew-up and moved out on their own,
Your husband passed away and you feel all alone.

You take it one day at a time,
Thinking your health is just fine,
Now you know that you were wrong,
and all your days just seem so long.

But then it happened, just out of the blue,
In walks your son, and his wife too,
Your daughter was behind with grandchildren galore,
as they place a wreath on your casket door.

Melissa Pardo
Age: 13

LOVE

Love is something special.
Nothing like anything on TV.
It's between a boy and a girl
or a man and a woman.
Now, it sometimes might lead to a marriage
or it might just lead to a friendship.
Now this needs to come to an end.

Ryan Alexandria Mackillop
Age: 8

ROCK OF LIFE

Rock of life
Bumpy, old
Buried in fresh, rich soil
A school yard
Kicked from one spot to another
Sparkles fade into black spots of age
continually stomped deeper and
deeper into the ground,
trying to get out
Crawling,
Never getting to the surface
Losing precious breath
Only to die and be replaced
by a more beautiful
Stone.

Marcia LaFrance
Age: 13

HAIR

Hair, Hair,
It's just not fair,
It never looks cool,
It makes you look like a fool,
It may curl,
You can make it whirl,
You think it looks like a blob,
But everyone says you did a good job.

Tammy Owen
Age: 11

PUPPIES

A puppy is in a pet shop whining pitifully,
Those sad brown eyes say 'please buy me'
A Doberman puppy across the street,
Yapping and howling to his own beat
A back yard puppy, happy as can be,
Bouncing around like she sat on a bee
Pekinese puppies eating beef chop suey,
It's just leftover from Wing Yee's
A poodle puppy named Frenchie,
Seeing the sights of 'Gay Paree'
All of these puppies are cute as can be,
But my peek-a-poo puppy is the one for me!

Jennifer Ernst
Age: 13

MY DOG SNUGGLES

Silly
Naughty
Unusual
Goofy
Gentle
Lively
Entertaining
Snugly

Catherine Srodawa
Age: 7

FORGOTTEN

Why do we forget the people of this war,
When everyone thought that there is no use
fighting for?
They sacrifice their arms, legs, and sometimes
their life,
When no one remembers them the rest of their
life.

I will not forget the heroes of this war,
The ones who fought for this great country,
To those people I will forget no more,
Because they fought for justice and liberty.

Brett A. Koenemann
Age: 14

SKIING

As we go down the slopes
I cannot help but to hope
For snowfall at night,
So there will be
More snow in the daylight.

Turning as I go
I attempt to follow the flow.
Over all the bumps and jumps,
I fly through the air,
And land on the snow.

Excitement swells in me
And increases as swift as can be.
After one final leap
The slopes began to get very steep.

Off to an icy trail I go
Between the trees
And on the snow.
With the sun
The trail glowed.

I decided that this would be the final run
And that I would return tomorrow
To have more fun.
With a smile on the way
So ended a perfect day.

Jeff Reed
Age: 13

IS IT SCARY IN THE DARK?

Is it scary in the dark?
Why of course it is don't be silly!
So many things in the dark
that give people the chilly willies!

Ghouls and ghosts and poltergeist,
flying through the air,
I don't know what to tell you,
just that they give me such a scare!

Bats and rats and big black cats,
goblins galore, nothing to adore,
and-a-knock-at-their-door.

Mitchell Stevens
Age: 9

COLORS

Pumpkins are
orange.
Cats are black.
When you see one
Please jump back.

Cindy Shoults
Age: 8

THE SKY IS BLUE

The sky is blue. It is pretty too.
The sky is blue with white clouds too.

I wish I could fly in the sky.
And sit on a cloud that is big and white.
It would be great to fly in the sky.
If only I could fly now!
Up in the sky would be great.

I could fly with the birds and the
bees, and butterflies too.

Katherine O'Neill
Age: 9

NO HOMEWORK

Today we have no homework.
Isn't that great? When we get home.
we get to jump around and play
....I can't wait, no math, no reading,
no spelling. How much fun will we have?....
There's no telling.
Now don't get me wrong, homework
can be good if it doesn't last too long.
So this is the end of my homework.

Melissa McGuire
Age: 8

ARTIST

The artist -
a wrinkly old man
with fingers
holding
gently onto the paintbrush

With brush in hand
palette full of paint
he
streaks
colors
over the canvas

His eyes -
two pools of paint
the color of the sky
red for his mouth
hair of black bristles

April Everett
Age: 9

BARK

Bark, bark, bark, bark, bark, bark, bark
Quiet--I just fed you!

Adrienne McDonald
Age: 11

WHO I AM

I am well in body,
　　but rumpled in spirit
I wonder about things to come
I hear the animals silent voices
I want the very best for myself
I am well in body, but,
　　rumpled in spirit

I pretend I am an artist,
　　painting on my expressions
I feel that knife
　　stabbing through my heart
I touch others feelings
I worry about our planets future
I cry silent tears
I am well in body,
　　but rumpled in spirit

I understand why our loved ones die
I say my feelings and thoughts
I dream of a cleaner, safer world
I hope 'we' wise up and take care
　　of our fragile earth
I am well in body,
　　but rumpled in spirit

Susan Desmond
Age: 13

THE GATES TO YOUR IMAGINATION

Gates to your imagination
   that's what they are.
They can take you to many places,
   both near and far.

But what are these gates
   that many have opened,
to explore this world,
   including its oceans?

You have probably used them
   often before,
to help and guide you,
   through life's door.

These gates are called books
   which many have found,
lead to adventures
   this wide world around.

So read each book
   with anticipation,
And you will expand
   your imagination.

David Broz
Age: 13

BLUE

Blue is the covers
that keep the world warm
It is the rivers and streams
which are emptied into
seas and oceans
Blue can be sadness
or a teardrop of joy
It's the whistle of wind
through the trees
And is a necessity of life

Scott Cole
Age: 13

THE FIREMAN

He walks with a great stride,
going towards the burning building.
He enters through the door,
beginning with his feet,
he feels a burning sensation
that slowly spreads to his whole body
He begins turning the color of fire,
in a matter of seconds he bursts into flames
Just adding to the rest of the
flaming burning building.

Tara Talia
Age: 13

DREAMS

As time goes by
It's like a dream in the wind.
Broken or lost,
Time will go by.

Dreams that are wanted,
Are gone and have perished.
Sadness is present,
As it comes over you.

But new dreams are formed
Each second of living.
New hope is built up,
You are living, still able.

Sarah Sherman
Age: 13

TOMORROW

The future that's unknown
Open for new ideas
Memories to build
Opportunities to take
Realizations to be accepted
Readiness to follow dreams
Only one chance to do things right
When tomorrow comes

Melanie Sampson
Age: 13

LOOKING BACK

The frail old lady slowly
 stepped down the road
Looking for the river where
 she used to catch frogs and toads
The river was not there -
 nowhere to be seen
The factory's smoke turned
 the grass brown and dead where
 it used to be green

She continued on down to look
 for the woods she used as a fort
Now that was replaced by a mall
 of some sort
As groups of people ran in
 and out
The bewildered old lady
 wondered what this generation
 was all about

She knew that nobody really
 cared
They just took out worthwhile
 places to put unnecessary
 establishments there

As the old woman left the place
 she grew up as a kid

She knew her childhood memories
were ruined because of what
some inconsiderate people did

Lindsay Deputat

DANCING

Dancing, dancing here and there,
Dancing, dancing everywhere.
I like dancing, yes I do,
Tap and jazz and ballet, too!

Erin Borowiec
Age: 9

CARNIVALS!

I like carnivals.
I like them a lot.
Especially when they're in the school parking lot.
With tilt-a-whirl which makes you twirl
A clown or two saying 'How do you do?'
The thunder bolt which gives you a jolt.
The merry-go-round with the cute sound.
Bumper cars going roar and of course a whole lot more!

Michelle Garrity
Age: 11

THE NIGHTMARE

The orange sky grew darker,
 as time quickly advanced.
I had no security except for
 the reassurance that the sun
 would soon rise again.
No where to run, Wherever I went
 it followed.
I cringed with fear,
 knowing it was there.
The thunder boomed
 to mark its presence
It was charging.
I was knocked down as it struck me.
Paralyzed, I lay there with beads of sweat.
Then I awoke to a sweet smell and a cool breeze,
 as butterflies danced above me.

Chris Chapple

MONTHS AND NUMBERS

April, May, June, July,
I will never tell a lie.
One, Two, Three, Four,
I will open up the door.

Ryan Bettelon
Age: 8

WINTER

Why is there a winter?
The pale sun reflecting on the snow
Is dull and colorless.
Wildlife and peoples' high spirits
Fade quietly with the warm summer weather.

Children slip and fall on ice,
And the roads are always dangerous.
Violent storms
Force people to stay indoors,
And no matter how much you 'bundle up',
The crisp wind chills you to the bone.

What is the sense of having snow,
If it never lasts?
A single snowflake;
A unique and beautiful creation,
Floats silently to the ground,
Only to melt.

An empty loneliness
Fills peoples' hearts,
Causing them to be
As bitter as a cold winter day.

Jennifer Kappler
Age: 13

CIRCUS

Circuses mean
Ice cream for you and me,
Roaring tigers,
Cool outfits and
Ugly elephants.
Seeing the circus is wonderful!

Rachel Murray
Age: 10

FEELING INSIDE

Sometimes I feel like a sailboat
    riding on the waves..
Sometimes I feel like a game
    always getting played..
Sometimes I feel like a snowflake
    slowly falling from the sky..
Sometimes I feel like a stereo
    being loud..
Sometimes I feel like a bad day
    waiting to happen..
Sometimes I feel like a football
    being kicked in the air..
Sometimes I feel invisible like
    no one sees me there..
My feelings inside
    are always different..

Rachel DiMassa
Age: 13

A GRAIN OF SAND

To see the world in a grain
of sand.
To hear the ocean by its
roaring waves.
To touch the daisies in the
wide open plains.
To hear the gentle blowing
wind.
To see the hills and the
mountainous land.
To see the world in a grain
of sand.

Carrie Sourbeck
Age: 11

GAR THE BEAR

We went to the fair
To see Gar the Bear
He was covered in hair
But his butt was bare
He gave a big scare
With his evil stare
Would you dare
See Gar the Bear?

Tinasha Pace
Age: 12

A RETURN TO WAR

Oh my, it's happened again.
We are in a war, but who will win?

Some maniac has caused a fight,
Laced with hate and anger and fright.

The fertile soil turns red with blood,
So many tears turn it into mud.

We will do what is assigned,
Though, it is wrong in many a mind.

So I'm a pilot in wartime flight.
It's my job, so I will fight.

A return to war is just like hell,
But it's my job, I'll do it well.

Great black clouds, they dot the land.
I hope the public will understand.

I'm just another killing machine,
Some people think it's very mean.

This battle is just insane.
A friend will die, I'll feel the pain.

I need some help to understand,
Why do we ravage this pleasant land?

They bomb us and we bomb them,
It happens time and time again.

But all is fair in love and war,
And so we'll fight and fight some more.

But what really troubles me,
And I think you'll all agree,

Why do old men send us off to fight,
While they are home at dawn's early light?

They are safe while we are slaughtered,
We'll never see new sons or daughters.

But, we'll still serve, protect and defend.
When will this insanity end?

Soon I hope and fervently pray,
For if not, 'twill soon come my dying day.

Michael Long
Age: 13

HOCKEY

H ockey is my favorite sport,
O r any kind of game.
C hanging it would be so bad; it wouldn't be the same.
K ind sports are not for me,
E ven sports that aren't so neat, but
Y et, as plainly you can see, HOCKEY'S still
    the sport for me!

Nicholas Cicchetti
Age: 10

UNITED STATES

The United States has been here long,
As long as a bird can sing a song.

It all started with a grain of sand
Now it is a grand ole land.

With all the stars in the sky
Every day can pass on by.

Making it through each day
Will be a brand new adventure in every way.

With a little love it will always
Be there to share.

SO CARE!!

Michael Flees
Age: 10

MATH

M ultiplication is my kind of thing.
A lways, always fun for me.
T hough at times it is hard to do.
H ope you can do it too!

Jennifer Cardamone
Age: 10

FRIENDS

Friends should stick together,
Because friendship is important.
No matter who you are,
Or where you are,
Everyone needs friends.
So now you've heard
Some reasons. Go get
Yourself a friend.
If you don't, you're
Missing out on a good thing.

Kimberly Griswold
Age: 10

THE MOON

The Moon is a ball of snow.
It is a bowl of mashed potatoes.
The Moon is a banana SOMETIMES
Or a huge candle.
Sometimes it is a half, as of a torn paper.
A shape of a face from a clock.
A giant pie floating in orbit.
Have you ever heard such nonsense?
That's the point of the Moon.
Can you imagine something like that?

Johanna Funaro
Age: 9

OCTOBER CHEER...

I'm stocking up on beef jerky.
But they're roasting a turkey.

I'm ready to play jokes on my boss,
While they're makin' cranberry sauce.

When I made my costume,
'Ha, Ha' said Tiffany Aostume.

Why aren't they trick-or-treating
with glee,
Instead of coming up and laughing
at me?

UH-OH! I feel like such a fool,
Tomorrow I'm not going to school.

I can't believe my eyes!
This thing took me by surprise!

I looked at my watch,
(I'm ready to burst)
I just realized

It is November the first!!!!

Sara Bryce
Age: 10

SEASONS

Winter, Summer, Spring and Fall,
They are seasons one and all.

Winter is my favorite season,
And here is my reason.
Winter always has snow,
And I get to drink cocoa.

Spring is a time for blossoms
You may even see some possums.
And if you look real thorough,
You may even see a burrow.

Summer is another season,
It's a season for some teasin'.
Swimming is really fun,
Just until Summer's done.

Fall is the prettiest season of all,
It is when the leaves begin to fall.
Red and yellow are what they become.
This is also know as Autumn!

Seasons come and seasons go,
It may rain and it may snow.
Through it all the months they pass,
Again another year at last.

Roni Coatley
Age: 10

NATURE

N ice and beautiful
A mazing
T rees
U nder the stars
R estful and peaceful
E agle

Craig Steiner
Age: 11

LIFE

Life is like a blooming flower,
Pretty sights off of a tower.
Life is as precious as some glass.
It's also precious when it's past.

Sometimes in life, you'll get mad.
Sometimes in life you'll be glad.

Treasure those memories and make
them last,
As you grow older, they will go fast.

So make your life the best it can be,
It will be great, just wait and see!

Devin Gray
Age: 11

YOU AND I, ME AND YOU

You and I, me and you
We are friends and that is true.

We play and play and play all day.
Until the day has come to say good-bye.

We say good-bye to each other,
And go home to our Father and Mother.

You and I, me and you
We are friends and that is true.

Courtney Allred
Age: 10

NATURE AND IT'S WORTH

Trees are umbrellas growing ever so tall.
Grass is like a jungle to ants that may crawl.
Rocks are shelter for beetles of sorts.
Water is a home for fish, maybe even resorts.
Flowers have pollen for a lot of bees.
People use nature's stuff, kill all it's worth
And tell a lot of bluff.

Gary Staten
Age: 10

THAT SILLY CAT

That silly cat wears my clothes around the
house. She wears this and that. Oh that
silly cat oh that silly cat, why does she
do that? What does she eat that makes her
do that? She twists and turns all night long.
And wags her super long tail.

Shannon McKinnon

NATURE

Grass is green
Bark is brown
Leaves are rough
Some are smooth.

In the winter, leaves fall off,
In the Spring they grow back on.

In the rain the mud is black
But in the sun the sand is very brown.

When the sun shines
And nature rolls on
Sticks grow long
When trees grow on
And that is all.

Jason C. Thompson
Age: 10

I made a rose so you could pick, I made grass
so you could feel, I made a chair so you
could sit, I made fruit so you could eat,
I made a rainbow so you could see,
I made a street so you could walk,
I made a car so you could travel.
But you did not pick my rose,
And did not feel my grass,
And did not sit in my chair,
And did not eat my fruit,
And did not see my rainbow,
And did not walk on my street,
And did not travel in my car.

Cory Cooper

FALL SUNSHINE

In the Fall the birds
Will fly, the sun will turn
Orange, and the leaves will change
And calmly fall to the ground.
They will blow away by the Fall
Breeze. Then when you wake,
Up in the morning you start
To worry that the beautiful
Colored leaves are covered
In snow.

Kristen Gillon
Age: 10

LOVER'S SORROW

Good-bye my love
For what might be
A sad prolonged eternity.
And though we shall be world's apart
You will always exist in my sweet heart.
For the moons shall rise and sun may fall
And night be summoned by the coyote's call
For the mountains may crumble to my feet
And the world may end in one heart-beat
But nothing will come between us.

Good-bye my love
For what might be
A sad prolonged eternity.
Though in another life
Some other day
In a kingdom far away
We shall meet again.

Go now, my love
For I cannot bear
To see again your loving stare
From eyes that will never meet mine again
From your face that I have known from way
   back when
We were in Heaven, up above.

I will always weep in this bed of sorrow,
Hoping for your return 'morrow
Good-bye, my love, forever.

Andrea Krantz
Age: 11

104

CHRISTMAS

C hristmas is the time of year.
H e was born the Christ of cheer.
R inging bells on Christmas day.
I n the sounds of holiday.
S inging silent songs of joy.
T en angels way up high.
M aking Christmas a lullaby.
A nd when you hear them sing songs of joy.
S end a message and tell him why because
   you love him and pray for him
   all the time.

Natalie Martin
Age: 9

THE SEASONS

Spring time brings us flowers.
Summer brings the sun.
Autumn brings us fallen leaves.
Soon cold dark winter days will come.
Then we'll look at the days gone by
And think of what we have done.
Have you helped someone along the way?
Or have you just had fun?

Lisa M. Visocchi
Age: 11

IF I WAS THE FIRST WOMAN PRESIDENT

If I was the first woman president
  I would be a good one
If I was the first woman president
  I would never be done being one.
If I was the first woman president
  I wouldn't take it as fun.
If I was the first woman president
  That would certainly be the day!

Lindsay Cachia
Age: 9

PARADISE COVE

Living on an island would be quite fun
Coconut bowling in the tropical sun
Living in palm tree condo with an ocean view
I'd have an iguana for a pet and playful
  monkey too
I would eat bananas for breakfast lobster
  for lunch
And in between I'd eat pineapple pizza for
  brunch
I bet you think this sounds pretty cool
But best of all there is no school

Grant Balogh
Age: 9

WINTER

Winter is a special season.
It comes every year for no special reason.
Snowflakes fall.
We make a snowball.
And have fun everyday in the winter.

Laura Allen
Age: 9

NATURE'S WAY

Nature has a wonderful way
to do things each and every day.
Snowflakes fall to the ground.
They break not a thing,
they make not a sound.
Flowers grow in the spring,
The trees sway, the birds sing.
The weather grows warm
and you can swim.
The bees produce honey]
and sing their hymn.
The leaves start to fall
and form a pile,
All these conditions make
you want to smile.

Mark Straub
Age: 11

SILLY BUTTERFLY POEM

Butterflies fly and flutter.
And they seem to fly like butter.

But then they would melt.
Just like busting your belt.

Aren't I silly?
I could name him Billy.

Stand by,
There's a butterfly!

Zachary Clancy
Age: 9

KITTENS

A kitten is like a little
ball of yarn rolling on the ground.

A nice fine silk blanket.

A kitten is a little snowball
in the middle of winter.

A kitten is a colored ball
of fur sitting on the floor.

Jason Unger

CHRISTMAS

Christmas comes when winters here...
Christmas comes once a year...
New Years comes when Christmas is done...
For another year!

Andrea Louise Perrin
Age: 9

MICE

Mice, mice, who likes mice?
They chew your dice, eat your sugar and spice

Mice sure aren't lazy.
They're so feisty they drive me crazy.

Mice come in different colors, but mostly
grime,
Which matches their daily crime.

You don't have to bribe mice to eat your
old rice.
You like mice?

Now here's some advice,
Go buy you some mice, but make sure
they're nice!

Leah D. Carty
Age: 11

WATCHING

In the window there she sits waiting very still.
She sits very still doesn't even look real.
Then she sees him sitting on a branch.
He doesn't move not even an inch.
Slowly she stalks him without a doubt
He can see her so he hops about.

Then 1 - 2 - 3-
Now she leaps for him but misses
Because she cannot get out!
Poor Sadie trapped inside longing to get out.

Heather McMahon
Age: 13

GIVE ME 1, 2, 3, 4, 5,

1, 2, 3, 4, 5
Give me 5 down low...
And, 4 let's go...
Give me 3 up high...
Give me 2...
Who has my shoe?
Said 2, 'Me'
Said 1, 'I do have my part'
'You're on!' said 2, 3, 4, 5
Give me 1...
Let's stop to run!

Natasha Dennis
Age: 8

HALLOWEEN

Somehow you live through it,
Not always sure you can do it.
You can't always keep your head,
Sometimes scares you right out of bed!

Can't dodge it,
Whole world's got it.

DANGER CONTAINS:
Black cats, werewolves,
Superstitions, spiders,
Nightmares, frightmares,
Vampires, witches.

Waiting, Waiting,
Few more HOURS,
MINUTES,
SECONDS!

Daylight comes,
Takes it away,
Forever to be gone,
Until .... Next Halloween Day.

Bethany Bray

SKIING

The snow lay on the ground like a blanket of light.
It almost hurt my eyes at the sight.

I looked at my brother ski with grace,
I said to myself, I'll ski the face.

The next hill we got to was so steep,
I left my family to ski the deep.

I was being chased by an avalanche,
I figured out I had no chance.

I was covered from head to toe,
So I dug myself out of the snow.

As I reached the surface,
I started to get nervous.

I couldn't find my parents,
So I looked for my brother, Clarence.

I saw my brother skiing in his big green
coat.
So, I yelled his name out in a beautiful
note.

Tyler Christensen
Age: 13

THE GRAND CANYON

How GRAND is the GRAND CANYON?
Is it GRANDER than the Grand Old Flag?
Is it GRANDER than the Grand Ole Opry?
Is it GRANDER than the Rio Grande?

How BIG is the GRAND CANYON?
Is it BIGGER than the BIG TOP CIRCUS?
Is it BIGGER than the BIG DIPPER?
Is it BIGGER than BIG FOOT?

How GREAT is the GRAND CANYON?
Is it GREATER than the GREAT LAKES?
Is it GREATER than a GREAT WHITE SHARK?
Is it GREATER than a GREAT OCEAN LINER?

Shawn Cool
Age: 13

MY BEAR

I have a favorite bear.
I always sleep with it.
Now the day is here to give it up...
I have to give it to my sister to keep
... I am very sad I want my
bear back.

Jacquelyn Storey
Age: 8

ME!

When I glance through my window,
all I see is rain.
When I touch my carpet,
all I feel is pain.
When I look at my room,
all I see is clutter.
When I touch my curtains,
all I feel is butter.
When I look at my walls,
all I see is writing.
But, when I look at my mirror,
all I see is me!

Kim Crabill

SANTA CLAUS

Santa Claus, Santa Claus
I was walking in the halls.
When I heard a reindeer breaking...
Reindeer laws!
So, I asked, 'What are Reindeer laws?'
My dad said, 'I don't know a thing about
Reindeer laws, so ask Santa Claus.'
'Santa Claus, Santa Claus.....'

Nicholas Norville
Age: 9

THERE IS NO LIMIT

I felt the cool air on my face,
As though I was in space;
I wish I was up flying around,
I wish I was up flying around,
But I was stuck, like glue, on the ground.

I wanted to be up where the sky is blue,
Instead of down here, tying my shoe;
I would love to fly around like a little pest,
Instead of taking my science test.

But I must take the test on mass,
If I wish to pass;
Even outside playing,
Would be better than staying in and
weighing;
So I took the test and to my surprise I got
an 'A',
And boy did that pay.

3.........6.........9.........
10 long years later,
I am not a singer, carpenter, or painter;
But an astronaut, and now I am finally going
into space,
With a helmet tight on my face;
I go up so high in the sky,

And now I really can.............FLY

Matt Sarkesian
Age: 13

CANCER

Cancer is a terrible thing
When someone knows someone else with it
No one's spirits ring

People cry
People sigh
And then
Maybe someone dies.

In the funeral home
People cry
But they are better when their family
is close by.

At the luncheon the people are very sad
But are glad when they know that he went
to heaven.

Then they go home and try to go to sleep
And in their bed they will weep.

And then there's a new day
And they try to forget about it on their way

People visit you
They talk to you
They comfort you
They make the pain go away.

Then through the year people cry
To help you, to comfort you
To make you feel all right.

Then you go to church one day
You pray extra hard for that person
And later that day something special happens
You get a special package, a special
compliment
And then you feel all right.

But then the next day something bad happens
Like someone getting sick
But then you pray and he feels better.

And in the next month or so you yourself
gets cancer
People pray a lot for you
And take you to the doctor's office.

And in his office he says:
You don't have cancer any more
And you feel very happy.
And then you think
Why wasn't he so lucky
Then you think some more
And decide he was, he got to go to heaven.

So there you see
How a story of cancer can be
Sad and happy.

Richard J. Petts
Age: 11

THE RIVER

Sometimes when I am sitting here watching the
    sun go down...
Looking at the river by the little tree house
    where the flowers are blooming
And the rain is still falling from the tree
    where the tree house was built
The sun has gone down and now you can see the
    shining blue water.
And, the water is sparkling blue...

Ashley Drain
Age: 8

SNOW

So white and beautiful as it falls to the ground,
So fragile and tender as it whittles around.

And just to think that no snowflake is alike,
Is just enough to give me a fright.

It sparkles and shines and is very bright,
As it falls in the hours of daylight.

Snow.
One day it's there and the next it's not.

Jason Gourley

THE TOY BOAT

There was once a little boy
Who wished to sail at sea
He thought there was, at the edge of the earth,
A land called Eternity.
So one day, he set out a small toy ship
Its fluttering sails bright green
Saying, 'Come back sometime, my little ship
And tell of all you've seen.'
He watched and watched the tiny boat
Until it sailed away.
Hoping that his precious boat
Would soon come back one day.
Months passed, years passed
In all, about seventy
And now the young boy was an old, old man
The ship gone from memory.
He sat at the shore of his old hometown
His happiness complete
When suddenly, disturbing peaceful thoughts
Something bumped his feet.
Scratched and scarred was his small toy boat
Returned to its master at last!
Fulfilling the dreams of a little boy
So long ago in the past.

Grace Lim
Age: 13

HUG ME, DON'T HURT ME

I looked, to you for comfort and love,
But received cutting words of discouragement
And ice filled tubs.

I dare not question your authority
for my burned, scared body can no longer
be covered by my clothes.
I ache not only from a sharp cold
blade, But from my bleeding heart
as it cries, 'OUT!' silently for help.

It shouldn't hurt to be a child
It shouldn't hurt to be a child
Hug me, don't hurt me.
Please hug me.
Please, please, please, don't hurt me.

Letrisha Rodgers
Age: 18

Where the winds blow;
And the birds call.
Where the waves crash;
And the sands crunch.
There on the seaside;
Again we shall meet.
And together we'll be,
Forever in time; so sweet.

Jennifer Williams
Age: 13

Ghosts are creepy,
Ghosts are queer.
I hate it when they howl in my ear!
And when I get sleepy,
And go to bed,
I hear ghostly noises in my head.

Jacquelyn Lozowski
Age: 9

3 SIMPLE STEPS TO A RECIPE FOR A FRIEND

First, you take a friend and put 'em in a bowl,
And mix it 'till you get to the North Pole.
Then you shape it into a BIG crescent roll.
And then you've finished your first goal.

Second, you sprinkle all of the things found in a friend.
Then you spread the yummy frosting on and blend.
Then, carefully place it in the oven, making
sure it won't bend.
And then you're almost to the end.

Third, you take the friend out of the oven
and let it cool.
Later you pry it out with a useful tool.
And stand it up right in a BIG pool.
What you have is not a fool, but a precious
jewel.
Now, you have finished the third rule.

Sesi Wong
Age: 13

OH, LITTLE KITTEN

She's a pouncy, flouncy, bouncy
    ball of fur,
Chasing bright balls of yarn
    and string.
Frisky little kitten, curling up on
    my lap,
Cuddly little fluff, that loves to
    purr.

Upon awakening she stretches and claws,
    my little kitten, a powderpuff ball.

As I lay awake at night I can hear
    her pawing at my door.
I can see her bright yellow eyes
    and can feel her soft wispy whiskers,
Oh, my little kitten that I simply adore.

Oh little kitten, cozy and warm,
    please stay with me until I'm full
grown.

Jonathan Morden
Age: 10

SUMMER DAY

Summer's colorful days
And the sun's bright rays.
Singing birds in trees,
And the buzzing bees.
Flying in the breeze,
These which make life beautiful,
Turn bad days into good.

School is out,
Fun is in,
And the weather is hot.

Aaron Mullins
Age: 10

THE SUN WORSHIPERS

Hundreds of mirrors in even rows.
Their reflective powers directing light and
    heat at a small point.
The raw earth cooked around the shadows of
    the solar field.

The sound of boiling water fills the air.
At the blink of an eye, field comes to life.
The clamor of engines pivoting the mirrors
    replaces the sound of water.
In an instant all is peaceful again.

Nathaniel Paul Merrell Riffe
Age: 12

NATURE SOUNDS

While I lay in my bed, in the morning
I open my window.
And I hear the trees shaking,
The birds waking.
I see the flowers blooming,
And the bees zooming by.
When the day has started
I think of what I can do,
Or what I want my day to be like.
Do I want it to be a good day, or a bad day?
While I sit in my room, I see the birds
soaring through the sky.
And I start to cry, and that is
My day.

Amy Burke
Age: 10

COMPUTERS

A computer is a robot with a smile.
It is a TV. that you work on for a while.
It is a memory machine.
A computer is a typewriter with a screen.
It is like a friend, it can help you think.
But sometimes I want to throw it in the sink.

Daniel M. Sporka
Age: 9

KITTENS

Fur soft as a bunny,
Ears, pointy as a pin,
Fur, fuzzy as cotton,
Cute as a teddy bear,
Purring like a motor,
Cuddly as a pillow,
Sweet as a baby,
They're friendly as can be,
I like them so much,
I have one of my own.

Christy Sokolowski
Age: 9

FOOTBALL

Running with the ball.
Trying not to fall.
Hearing the fans heckling.
Waiting for my name to
be called.
James Torres, get out
there and hit.
We want a victory!!
Don't ever quit!

James A. Torres
Age: 9

I LOVE NATURE...

As I was walking down the street,
I realized that nature is very neat.

In the magnificent trees,
You can see the hardworking bees.

The tiny ants on the street,
Just love to crawl around my feet.

In the spacious, blue sky,
The various birds love to fly.

The refreshing, clear waters,
Are the homes for fish and otters.

Nature is not just made of creatures,
There are countless other features.

I love the rolling, green plains
And the showering, sprinkling rains.

The tall, shady trees
Provide a calm, gentle breeze.

The spectacular, sandy beaches are
a good place to relax,
I just love them up to the max!

The sparkling stars at night,
Oh! What a breath-taking sight!

But I think that the most spectacular

thing,
Is us, the human being.

Amy Patel
Age: 10

THE MAIDEN

In a cottage deep in the forest, lives a
maiden.
With many jobs and chores, she is laden.
She draws her auburn hair into a bun,
to keep it out of the way, until her chores
are done.
She gathers food for the ducks who live
nearby,
if she doesn't feed them, they will cry and
cry.
Then she's in her cottage to sweep with her
broom,
Waiting for her next, is her weaving loom.
She weaves for the old and poor in town,
She stuffs pillows out of the duck's down.
This good maiden is clean and pure as a
dove,
Because she has something special, that is
known as love.

Sarah Lomas
Age: 13

THE RIVER

The River runs black and cold,
   Surrounded by timber from trees of old.
In my memory I will hold,
   The River that runs black and cold.

This River I see is filled with gold,
   And on it's shore stands a bird so bold.
This bird is wise so I am told,
   Along this River that runs black and cold.

The River today might be old,
   and the land might be sold.
But in my memory I will hold,
   The River that runs black and cold.

Travis Robert Gottlin
Age: 11

AUTUMN DAYS

When the wind blows, when leaves
scatter, when the tree's leaves are
a rainbow, when a chill blows over
the hill, when you wear a coat,
when mountain goats jump up and
down the hill,
It's autumn!

Carlin Danz
Age: 8

IF I WERE IN CHARGE OF THE WORLD

If I were in charge of the world I would
protect wildlife, hoping that the numbers
would increase.
There'd be no such thing as violence or
crime.
Parents wouldn't be allowed to refuse
anything their children wanted.
Children would be allowed to drive as soon
as they can reach the windshield at the
same time.
Everything would be free, especially the
most expensive products on the market today.
All desserts that taste good would be
counted as vegetables and we would have to
eat them everyday.
There'd be only 1 day of school a month.
All historical objects would be left alone.
All homeless people would have a home.
There'd be no pollution.
Wars would never start.
All people and animals would live forever.
There wouldn't be any bad drivers.
I'd ban fighting and drugs.
In school you wouldn't have homework.
I would be able to do magic with the snap
of my fingers.
Nobody would need special education.

Kerrie Lemerand
Age: 9

REMEMBRANCE

There was a time when I served my country,
Over there I was hailed as a hero,
but here I was treated as an outcast.
I expected to return to cheering crowds.
Instead I received boos and hisses.
The government was supposed to repay me
for my valor,
Medical care, housing, income.
All they gave me was the brush off.
So, now I eat, sleep, and live in this
homeless shelter.
The government says that people like me are
rare, but I know otherwise.

Phillip Kennedy
Age: 13

LONELINESS

A boy sits in a corner
His parents left a week ago and haven't
come back.
He gets swallowed in his tears and sorrows.
The rooms seem to close in on him.
The room fills with blackness, the color of
his parents hearts.
He becomes lost in the cold murky depth.

Michael Keefe
Age: 13

REMEMBRANCE

Red, yellow, orange, just a touch of brown,
The leaves decorate the small, antique town.
The canvas of dirt roads and large gleaming
fields,
Here what the leaves had rested on when
they finally came to yield.
The brilliant leaves were what was left
From the once colorful trees.
But now all that's left are the visions
of you and me.

Grant Griffith
Age: 13

The sun shines bright,
the wind blows light.
Flowers bloom nice and slow,
in the garden little and low.
Animals run and play,
across the grass and they will go,
never stopping in the snow.
Seasons come and go,
as we rake leaves and shovel snow.
Nature is a cool thing,
just like saying Cing Bata Bing.

Tanya Jolly

THIS IS A HORRIBLE HABALOOBIE

Habaloobies hang out in hallway habitats
that have hampers, hammocks, and halfhearted
half sisters. Hallway habitats are hauled
from house to house in Harrisburg.

Habaloobies eat hamburgers, hard boiled
eggs, Hallmark cards, Hungry Howie pizza,
and hairbrushes with helpings of hairspray.

Habaloobies like happy hamsters, healthy
hedgehogs, and hesitating hillbillies.
Hebaloobies like having harmless hippos
hula-hoop on holidays.

Habaloobies are hazardous, heart broken,
hockey players who do history homework on
Honolulu. Habaloobies have hopeless
horoscopes and wear hoopskirts to
horrify horses.

This horrible Habaloobie handed out hot
dogs to me on a houseboat on the Hudson
River. However, it humiliated my husband
Harry while hurrying over the hurdles
at a historical high school in Houston.

Sarah Scherdt
Age: 13

Gold pagans of Peru
Chanting death songs,
Piercing Spanish eardrums.
Rattling the Spanish minds,
With a high pitched sound.

The fiercest warriors,
In the world
Trembling
Urinating with terror.
Doomsday is upon them.

The mighty Spanish,
Terrorized by an unseen army
Of lost and abandoned souls.
Hypnotic Peruvians, misguided
by a young sun's feebleness.
Falling prey to Spanish wit
and superiority.
Native bare bodies falling lifelessly
to pools of denied blood.

The Spanish with another victory
of deceit and greed.
The minds intent on killing
And not on reasoning.

Todd Luckhardt
Age: 14

I MADE

I made the trees,
the sun,
the sky.
I made the tears that you cry.
I made the earth that you walk on.
I made the tunes for your songs.
I made the rivers,
the lakes,
the seas.
I made the forest, the forest green.
I made the mountains,
the hills and rocks.
I made the clouds, way at the top.
I made all of the things that you see.
And I made them to last for eternity.

Lauren E. Atkins
Age: 10

STARS

Stars are very pretty at night.
Stars glitter very bright.
Stars help the moon glow right.
Stars are even like a night light.
Stars help you see in the dark,
dark night.

Heather Schwochow
Age: 8

SPRING

Spring
warm, sunny
rain brings flowers
beautiful setting evening skies
growing

Kristen Dudak

CAN'T HIDE IT ANYMORE

There are feelings I just can't hide,
Feelings of emptiness inside.
Everyone just makes it worse.
They don't know how much it hurts.
I may seem like I really don't care,
But I really hurt; you must be aware.
People treat me likc I'm a real dummy,
I may laugh, but it's really not funny.
One little joke about me is okay.
But people continue and get carried away.
I feel like my reputation is buried in dirt
What does a little dizziness hurt?
I know I'm known as 'Hall' and 'Light Post'
And that, of all things, hurts the most.
So, people, I'm finally bringing it out,
That isn't what I'm all about!

Rhiannon Rust
Age: 14

FALLING RAIN

Rain, rain falling down.
Hits softly in the puddles,
All around the ground.

Kristopher Lien
Age: 9

HOMEWORK

Homework, oh homework; I hate you so!
Why I have so much of you I do not know.
You ruin my week nights,
and get me grounded off the phone.
I can't help it, but when I see you I grumble
and I moan every night I work,
work, and work some more.
I write 'til my fingers are numb and sore.
Homework, oh homework, I guess I can't
complain for if I didn't know you I'd
probably be insane!
When I see you I want to pull my hair out.
When I think about you I want to scream
and pout.
I can't wait 'til the day
I never see you again.
About seven or eight years, maybe even ten!
Who knows, it depends.

Tracey Russell
Age: 11

WEEPY FEELINGS

In the dark cold night,
Night owls sing as shadows run.
Where are the shadows.

Stephenie Ireland
Age: 9

THE GRUESOME GHOUL

Gruesome Ghouls live in gross garbage cans
on George School.

Gruesome Ghouls gobble grapes, gator guts,
gooey goobers, gold goblets, and garlic.

Gruesome Ghouls like to gamble, give
goose bumps to girls in Greece, get a good
giggle after going to the ghoul ghost
house, and give guys gourmet goodies.

Ghouls give gossip, grow giant grasshoppers,
give gloves to glowing glass, and eat
goulash.

This ghoul made me go up a great grapevine
and gulp a geyser.

Rachael Hawkins
Age: 13

The clouds are real dark.
The rain is starting to fall.
Knocking at my door.

Amy Lawson
Age: 9

LOVE

Love is something
that takes you
outside in the
freezing cold.

Love makes all
people feel like gold.

Love makes new
friends feel like old.

Love always makes
you feel bold.

Love is everything as
you can see.

Love created you
and me.

Sarah Hughes
Age: 8

HOME SWEET HOME

The snow is falling.
The bears are hibernating.
The ground is like home.

Anthony Westenbarger
Age: 10

CATS, CATS, CATS

Cats are playful,
Cats are fun,
Cats are always on the run.

They sneak around,
They jump about,
They're happy when you let them out.

Cats can come in all shapes and sizes,
They're furry, they're fluffy,
and some are quite puffy.

They purr, they meow,
They drink milk from a cow,
They eat and they sleep,
and they don't earn their keep.

That is the life of Cats, Cats, Cats.

Meaghan McLaud

THERE'S A MONSTER UNDER MY BED

There's a monster under my bed
Yes, I know it's there
It wants to eat me for dinner,
Because it's probably the size of a bear

It's got big eyes and is completely green
It's the ugliest thing you've ever seen
If you were walking down the street
It's not the guy you'd want to meet
There's a monster under my bed
It really likes to eat
But it probably wouldn't like me
I bet it wouldn't like things sweet!

Katie Rusinko

MY NOSE

I found a lampshade.
I found a troll.
I found a catfish.
I found a pole.
The pole hit me, so I am told.
It turned my nose into rosy gold.
Sometimes I shiver to think what else
  it might deliver.

Robin Buchbacher
Age: 8

Flowers
elegant, soft
bloom, simple, gentle
feeling of absolute beauty
blooming

Kim Strauch

FOOTBALL OT

On September 21 there was a football game
It was U of M vs. Notre Dame
One was a top team in the Big 10
But the other one could have never been

For some reason it was cold that day
As U of M tried to keep ND out of their way
U of M was hoping to go to the Rose Bowl that year
But Notre Dame thought that was quite queer

By the second half Michigan had one TD
And guess who it was scored by -- yep, Tyrone
Wheatly

With about two minutes left in the second half
Alexander caught his first touchdown pass
The score remained tied at 17
And the game was over because there is no OT

Mike Krueger
Age: 13

Spring
warm, colorful
lawns being mowed
cheers up one's spirit
green

Christa Corwin

THE LIFE OF JESUS

Jesus' birthday is in December,
  that is the day that we should remember.
Jesus was born in a manger,
  then the animals kept him out of danger.

One day his parents took him to the temple,
  to them he was a very good example.
He started off as a young teacher,
  there they found him teaching teachers.

When he was older he died for us,
  the way he dies was on a cross.
They buried Jesus in a tomb,
  but in three days it was an empty room.

He arose from the dead that third day,
  He was alive in a real way.
In forty days he went up to His Father,
  life after that for Him was no bother.

Mary Anne Potok
Age: 11

Gymnastics
fantastic, enjoyable
flip, tumble, run
feel your heart soar
acrobatics

Autumn Howe

CHEETAH

There once was a cheetah
Who's name was Letta.
He ran very fast
And never came in last.
They gave him a trophy
made of gold.
He promised that it would
never be sold.

Anthony McGraw
Age: 8

DREAMING

When stars rise in the sky,
And my family's in bed,
And the sun has gone away,
Dreams fill up my head.

Suddenly I'm in the woods
Walking with a unicorn.
On my head there is a crown,
On his - a golden horn.

Then I'm in a spooky house,
Shivering with fear.
Forgetting that I'm dreaming,
I think my time is near.

Next, I'm floating on a cloud,
Then on the shining sea,
But when I wake up in the morning,
No one will believe me.

It's good to wake up knowing
That everything's all right.
But though I've had some fearful times,
I can't wait until the night!

Amy Hosner
Age: 11

THE DOVE

There once was a dove that was fine and I
always called her mine. Then all of a sudden,
she was free. Then once again she was mine.

Courtney Fahlen
Age: 11

APPLE

There was an apple on the tree.
Waiting there for me to see.
He seemed to wink and shine at me.
On that was a glee for me to see.
Then a bee hit me on the knee.
And the apple fell from the tree.
Then there was no apple for me to see.

Jennifer Heron
Age: 8

THE MANATEE

Floating in the deep canals
Out into the sea,
Near the piers and boating docks,
He seems quite large to me.

Such a harmless peaceful creature
Doesn't need to be disturbed.
Why people keep on killing them
Has me quite perturbed.

Feeding on the ocean's plants,
Coming up for air,
His gentle ways and numbered days
Leave my heart most bare.

Florida has respect for him
And tries to save his life,
But it is an endless battle
And an awfully weary strife.

Someday they will all be extinct,
Left no more to roam,
Washing up on ocean's banks
With all the filthy foam.

Traci Faulkner
Age: 11

JAKE THE SNAKE

His name is Jake the Snake.
He shakes rattles and rolls,
He ate all my trolls.

I don't know how he found
them hiding in the hole,
his head covered with a bowl.

He is not my kind of guy,
Eating every fly that passes by
in the sky.

Ryan Pruente
Age: 8

NATURE

Look at a tree
  What do you see?
What have you heard
  about a bird?
Look at a leaf
  Does it cause you grief?
Feel the air
  as it blows through your hair.
These are some gifts of nature!

Kyle Rose
Age: 11

SEASONS OF THE YEAR

During spring
Birds sing,
Leaves grow,
And animals scurry out of their burrows.
Crops are planted,
Seedlings spring,
And thunder cracks to make your ears ring.

During summer
Children hardly slumber,
Because they want to play
All through the day.
The grass is growing now,
And so are the apples. (Wow!)
Animals scatter,
As the ball is thrown to the batter.

Fall finally arrives,
And what a surprise,
To see all the leaves turn
Different colors to beautify.
The weather is cooling,
Yet still very hot.
And school is starting,
When people think it should not.

Winter is here,
Let's all give a cheer,
To say good-bye to hot weather,
Hello to the cold winds and snow.
Children run outside,
And onto the ice they slide.
While snowmobiles are getting all fixed up,

Grownups sit around with a hot chocolate cup,
Sitting in their cozy seats
Eating all their Christmas treats.

Renee Kramer
Age: 12

Winter has come
I'm ready for fun.
Let's play in the snow,
We can slide jump and run,
We'll have to hurry to beat the sun.

Marcie Harris
Age: 8

GOD'S BEAUTY

The churning leaves begin to land.
Bright colors whip around like blowing sand.
Red leaves stand out from the others,
as one falls, then another.
Orange leaves look like the bright gold sun,
and as the wind blows they
tumble one by one.

Cristina Kramer
Age: 12

CLOUDS

The clouds are sad when
they are gray, and when they are blue
they are happy.
In the winter the clouds are full of snow.
In the fall the clouds are crying with tears.
In the spring the wind pushes the clouds
very fast.
In the summer there is lots of thunderstorms
and rainbows.

Marek Sawicki
Age: 7

A FRIEND

A friend is someone who cares for you,
There's lots of things a friend will do.
A friend will always be around.
Especially when you're feeling down.
You will always enjoy the time you share.
You and your friend can go anywhere.
A friend will always be real true.
And cheer you up when you're feeling blue.

Robyn English
Age: 10

NATURE

Nature is a beautiful thing
Winter, summer, fall, or spring.
Just look out your window and there you see
A pretty flower, a bumblebee and maybe even
    a palm tree.
Winter is full of piles of snow.
Summer is abundant of sunshine aglow.
Fall has lots of colorful leaves.
Springtime will always make you sneeze.
Now I have given you some of the reasons
You should enjoy all of the seasons.

Sarah LeAnn Weber
Age: 10

When I go
Up north, I like to
Play in the woods every day.
The trees I climb in the breeze sway
back and forth and make me sneeze.
When I'm done, I go inside
And find a good
place
to
hide.

Michael Sliger
Age: 9

LOST LOVE

I didn't mean to lose you.
I didn't see you go.
I should of went to.
I should of said yes instead of no.
I should of let you know
That I never really wanted you to go.
I wonder if you think about me
if only you could see you never
even knew how much you meant to me.
A phone call from your mom
she tells about a lake
this must be some kind of mistake.
She tells me that you're hurt
She tells me that she's sad.
I call you every single day
I just can't keep the tears away.
Why don't you answer the phone
maybe you're just not home.
Go to the hospital, doctor tells me
suicide in his sleep he must of died.

Dobbie Bacon
Age: 11

TRUE FRIENDSHIP

Through good times and bad,
Through thick and through thin,
When I didn't belong
You helped me fit in
You gave me a peace
In a world strange to me
Your sweet smiling face
Was all I could see
In a world full of frowns
Your laughter came through
And that's when I found
A friend that was true

Joy Harvey
Age: 13

Little statue short and grand,
Sitting on a little stand.
Hoping to see a little hand
With some copper or some silver.
Oh, how silver makes me quiver.
My father once told me of a
coin worth a dollar.
Yes, that was said by my father.
It hits the water with a great ker-plunk.
You get them about once a month.
So here I stand short and grand
Waiting for that little hand.

Amie Paulson
Age: 11

TO SOMEONE WHO CARES

To someone who cares, My life is full of
puzzling errors.
To someone who cares, My guilt is hard
to bear.
To someone who cares, My feelings are
shredded with tears.
To someone who cares, Trouble gets piled
up in pairs.
To someone who cares, My soul burns from
bad affairs.
To someone who cares, Life isn't fair.
To someone who cares, It is as noticeable
as a King's trumpet flares.
That no one cares!

David Hudnall
Age: 12

MY MOTHER MADE ME

My mother made me kiss Aunt Dee,
My mother made me sing with glee,
My mother made me eat an anchovy,
My mother made me wear a dress, oh yes,
My mother made me build up stress,
My mother made me do a chore,
What are mothers really for?

Lindsey Marie Bobay
Age: 10

JACK

There once was a mouse named Jack, who
lived in a potato sack. He played with a
hat, Then played with a cat. And that was
the end of poor, poor Jack.

Amie Most
Age: 11

LEAVES OF AUTUMN

Leaves of autumn, red and blue. Leaves of
autumn old and new.
Leaves of autumn, green and gold. Leaves of
autumn strong and bold.
Leaves of autumn on tree or ground. Leaves
of autumn tremble sound.

Betsy Venturino
Age: 11

AUTUMN

Leaves are fun in Fall.
Soft leaves blowing in the wind.
Whispering in my ear.

Kara Yarnall
Age: 8

DEER

The deer on our farm,
They romp and play,
As they eat all the apples
And most of the hay!

We see them at dusk,
We see them at dawn,
As the Does and their Fawns
Crossing our lawn.

The buck's antlers
Grow big and tall,
As the weather changes
From summer to fall.

I hope that they stay
And play for days,
As they bring joy to
Our brisk Autumn Days.

Blake Eavenson
Age: 8

Kitty, kitty, drinking milk;
Kitty, kitty, your fur's like silk.

Kitty, kitty, you don't like lightning;
You think the sound of thunder's frightening.

Kitty, kitty, I love you so,
Even though the thunder goes!

Kitty, kitty, now that you've died
I'll sit by your grave and say you're alive!

Brittany Stedman
Age: 7

A little bird told me the day
would bring sunshine, laughter and fun.
Boy, it's fun playing in the sun.
But, on the way, rain will come today.
The sun will be hiding behind the clouds;
the thunder is roaring loud.

The bird flies to his nest and lands
and takes a rest.
The sun comes out.
The bird's in a tree.
He is happy and says to me,
'I am happy and you should be.'

Jamie Wimble
Age: 7

THERE WAS A FLOWER

There was a flower
That I planted.
It grew so tall,
It grew so tall . . .
That I had to get rid of it!

Megan Frantz
Age: 7

CAN I

Can I, Can I, Please, Please, Please.
I promise I'll eat all my peas.
I'll make my bed and clean my room,
If I can't it will be my doom.
I really, really have to do it,
Please can I get my mitt.
I have to, I have to,
Who can stop me but you?
Please, Please, Please!
You know I'll eat my peas
And make my bed and clean my room.
It really will be my doom.
I really, really have to do it.
Please, Please, Please can I get my mitt.
Can I, Can I, I Can! I Can!
Thank you! Thank you, I won't do it again!

Kristin Slattery
Age: 9

MY CAT

My cat is orange and white.
A shadow in the night.
His eyes are gold.
And he's four years old.
Because his rear end bobbles;
My cat's name is Wobbles.
I really hate
When he chases me at a fast rate.
Then he catches me and bites.
Holding on to my leg tight.
I continue on walking cautiously
While he convenes restlessly.
When I get to my bed,
He lays down near my head.
But in the morning when I wake up,
He starts playing again
Just like a pup.

Stephen O'Neil
Age: 13

Fall, fall is so fun. I love fall,
fall is done.
Boo hoo, boo hoo!
But I do not like it when fall is done.
I do not like it when fall is done.

Danielle Courtney
Age: 8

Winter is a time of beauty and cold
The might of a snowstorm
A friend's hand you hold.

Winter is white
With globs of fluffy snow
And the beauty found outside
Should never have to go.

For winter is filled
With hardships and cheer
But to me cold winter
Is the best time of the year.

Kimberly Henry
Age: 10

WHILE LIGHT SNOW

Icicles cool and wet
Santa and the elves are working in the night
As the snowman comes alive
Icicles cool and wet
Little bites of snow on the Christmas tree.
Angels flying white as snow
As Santa flies away
Icicles cool and wet
Holly hanging from the ceiling its berries
    red & bright
As the snow drifts in the cool wet night

Michelle Lorraine Reno

The pilgrims suffered hardship
No laughter or cheer
But when they got together
They had the best time of the year.

Thanksgiving is made up
Of laughter and joy
Of warmth and friendship
Felt by every girl and boy.

On Thanksgiving night
As we eat and say grace
We must remember the people
Of the early race.

Kori Henry
Age: 12

LOVE

Love can be special.
Love is true.
Love is for everyone
Me and you.
So share your love
Because love is free
For it is better to give
Then it is to receive.

Elizabeth Beck
Age: 10

Fish
colorful,
exuberant
bite my hook
steaming on my plate
yum

Erin Yoho

Mom and Dad stayed in bed
In fact, everyone did.
It wasn't till ten o-clock
my dog came and woke me up.
I ran down the stairs and
leaped on the couch. I.
couldn't believe the sight, I
saw it was such a beautiful
scenery.

Molly Cassidy

PIRATES

P irates steal the treasure.
I slands are their favorite spots to hide.
R ad reptiles rule the land
A nd when
T he captain gets grouchy
E verybody hides, everybody
S aid 'how rude!'

Hannah Prohaska
Age: 9

CHRISTMAS

Christmas sour, sweet
Snowballs are something children eat
Outside the snow is frozen
While diamonds land on people's
noses.
Outside trees are old
I think I better go in
I have a cold.

Curlisha Creighton
Age: 9

SHARK

I went to the ocean
to find a shark.
When I got there it
was too dark.
It looked like it was
storming.
The waves, they were
forming.

David M. Gray
Age: 9

THE NOISY DARK NIGHT

When I lay in bed it's very dark
Sometimes I hear the neighbor's dog bark.
I try to listen to all the alley cats.
I even named them Smokey, Tom and Bats.
I live somewhere very, very noisy,
About 25 miles East of Boise.
I think I'll have to count sheep,
So I can finally fall asleep!

Devon Paige Casady
Age: 10

A METEOR

A meteor is like a comet
flying through the air.
A meteor is like a train's
brakes throwing hot sparks
every which way.
A meteor is like the sun glowing
bright red while speeding as
fast as a bullet.

Justin Washburn
Age: 10

Spring
rainy, fresh
starting over again
new creatures being born
beginning

Erin Purdy

BOB'S CORN

There once was a man named Bob. Who couldn't
eat corn on the cob. So then his wife gave him
a knife and Bob cut the corn off the cob.

Jason Emmendorfer
Age: 11

Space
black antigravitational
filled with stars
full of unanswered questions
infinite

Ben Strickland

Mountains
formidable, rocky
replenishing the sky
they fill my eyes
hills

Deanna Dunham

Soccer
Muddy and fun
Referee, out of bounds
Goalie, kick, net, forward, defense
Winner

Patrick Miller
Age: 11

A cheetah
on a gloomy night
in a dark and spooky forest
leaping through the weeds looking
for food

John May
Age: 11

Balloon
Red thick
tossing twisting spinning
flies like a helicopter
ball

Amal Taleb
Age: 8

Balloon
round rubbery
twisting glowing turning
like a lost ball.
ball

Mona Aljahmi
Age: 8

Air
Damp, Dry
Blowing, moving, pushing,
Dry as a dog's biscuit
ozone.

Ryan Wojtyna
Age: 8

Eye of an alligator
Eye of a dog
Turn my brother
Into a frog.

Kendra Simonds
Age: 10

WINTER

During the winter
the ground is all white. It is
extremely pretty.

Cindy Marie Cattier
Age: 9

SILENT NIGHT

The water is still
The sun fades to red and orange
Birds fly everywhere.

Sarah Overmyer
Age: 9

CURTAIN CALL

The sun sets in the
distance, lighting up the sky
with lovely colors.

Matt Messink
Age: 9

TREE

Outside my window is my TREE.
Blowing its leaves at me.
Making it as cold as can be.
Do you have a tall tree like me?

Austen Pasley
Age: 8

MONSTERS

Once I saw a monster head
That came out of the ground.
He came over and said,
'I want, I want my PUMPKIN HEAD.'

Ryan Johnson
Age: 9